Bob

The Short Life of Robert John Mutton

Bob – The Short Life of Robert John Mutton

Copyright 2023 Peter James Bond and Graham Himmelhoch-Mutton

PO Box 964
ROSNY PARK 7018
Tasmania
Australia

www.pjbond.com

ISBN 978-0-6487713-5-7

All rights reserved. No part of this publication may be reproduced, stored in a retrieval system, or transmitted, in any form or by any means, electronic, mechanical, photocopying, recording or otherwise (except under the statutory exceptions provisions of the Australian *Copyright Act 1968*) without the prior written permission of the publisher.

Bob

The Short Life of Robert John Mutton

PETER JAMES BOND, PUBLISHER
PO BOX 964, ROSNY PARK 7018, TASMANIA, AUSTRALIA

For Mary, Andrew, Brian and Cameron

Contents

	Preface	6
1.	Mutton Family History	7
2.	Bob's Story – England	11
3.	Bob's Story – Australia, Hobart and Launceston	21
4.	Bob's DX History	43
5.	Bob's Story – Australia, Sydney	46
6.	Of Planes, Radios and Automobiles	53
7.	9th August 1977	56
8.	Some Random Memories	58
9.	A Final Word from Mary	62
10.	A Final Word from Bob	63
11.	Some Random Photos	64

Preface

This small volume is a tribute to Robert John Mutton, universally known as Bob. His father, Eric John Mutton, self-published his memoirs in 2002. These were republished in 2012 and again in 2021. The last volume was an expanded Centenary Edition on the occasion of what would have been his 100th birthday. The previous year, we published a similar, albeit smaller edition for our mother, Irene Emily Louise Mutton. 2020 would have been her 100th birthday.

Bob was born in 1947, so 2022 marked what would have been his 75th birthday. That year also marked 45 years since his passing, in Sydney, in 1977. For the benefit of family members and perhaps some old friends, this book presents the abbreviated story of his all-too-short life.

It is fortunate that Eric did compile his memoirs, as Bob's early years might otherwise remain unknown to most people. We, his surviving brothers, were eight and 14 years younger. Our memories of Bob are therefore constrained by this timeframe.

Of the many photos presented here, some of the early ones have been digitally colourised. However, not all images lent themselves successfully to that technology, and we offer those in their original glorious monochrome. Rendering colour from greyscale delivers realistic, though not always historically accurate results. Apologies for any errors!

Peter Bond
Graham Himmelhoch-Mutton
February 2023

◆

1. Mutton Family History

Tracing a family tree is a fascinating exercise made simple with online resources. However, it can also be frustrating when research into a particular thread draws a dead-end or ambiguities. Eric started the process many years ago when research demanded visiting archives or engaging researchers overseas. Using Eric's early work, Graham and Peter expanded the Mutton family tree using Ancestry and MyHeritage.

Understandably (perhaps), Eric concentrated on the Mutton line, though the Morris tree is just as important. A research difficulty is that Morris is a common name in England, and one must be careful that likely returns are accurate. Our Mutton family tree is advanced, dating back to the 1700s. The earliest name on the Morris side also dates to the 1700s. However, this is the maternal side of Irene's family tree, the Buckland line. Drawing a family tree becomes more complicated as you research deeper in time. It can, occasionally, seem like an infinite diverging regress.

Happily, Bob started his own family tree research, finding the earliest record of the Mutton[1] name as 1195. While he left behind no research documents, he did secure a coat of arms[2]. This is safely held in the family archive. The year 1195 should be regarded only as indicative, not definitive.

The two-headed eagle symbolises conjoining forces. The cinquefoil (five-leaved) indicates hope and joy and represents a flowering plant of the rose family. The colour argent (silver or white) means peace and prosperity, while gold (or yellow) denotes generosity and elevation of the mind.

Forebears of the Mutton family made their way to England after the Norman Conquest in 1066. However, if this is a separate family line, the name would be an Anglicised reference to the Moutons of Normandy. In modern French, mouton translates as sheep, but in the 11th century, the language spoken in Normandy was Old Norman French. Therefore, this regional dialect may have assigned a different meaning.

The name varies in spelling (see footnote) as, in the 12th century, standardised written English was some way into the future. Thought to

---

1 Variations of the name Mutton include Muton, Mytton, Myreton, Myrton, Mouton, Myttins, and Mitton.

2 At least one authority indicates there is no such thing as a family crest and that coats of arms belong to individuals, not entire families.

Mutton Family Tree

Genealogical research for English families can be a simple process from 1837 when general records were established. Prior to that, separate parish records must be studied. From Australia that can be difficult. Other researchers have identified Samuel Mutton's father as another Samuel, born about 1770, though no documentary evidence has not yet been sourced.

Chart 1

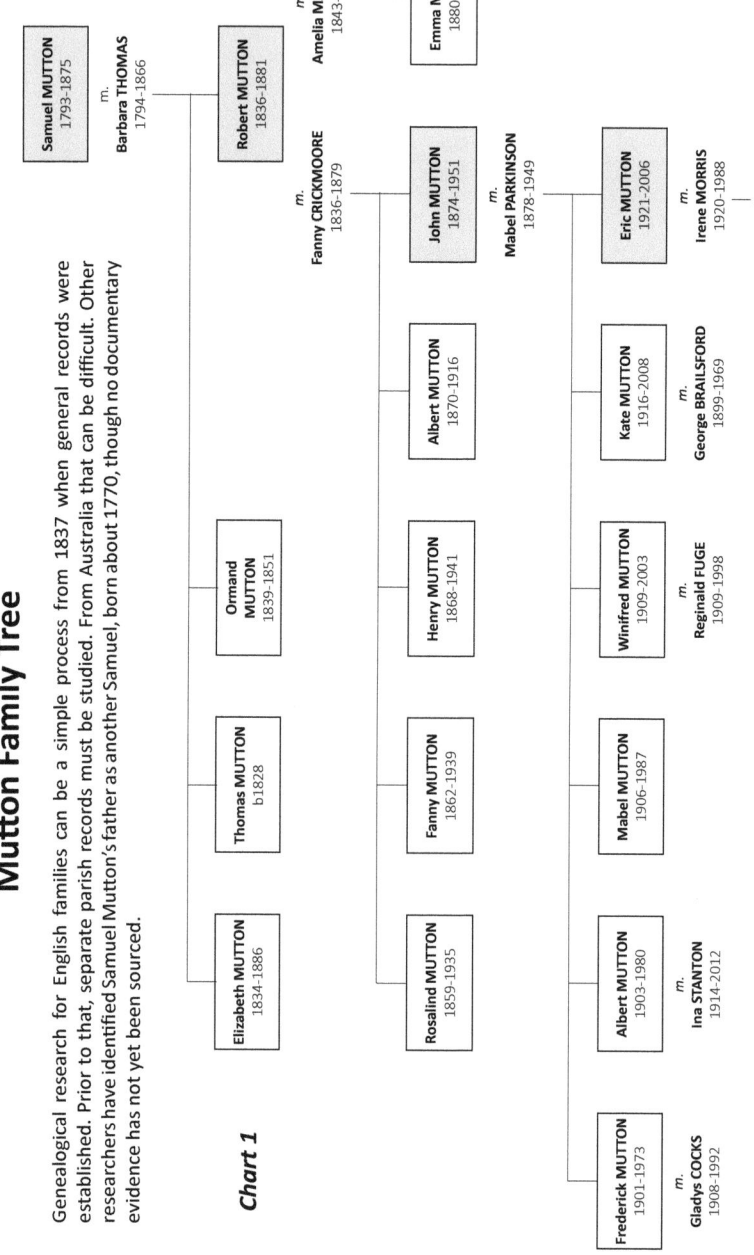

Bob – The Short Life of Robert John Mutton

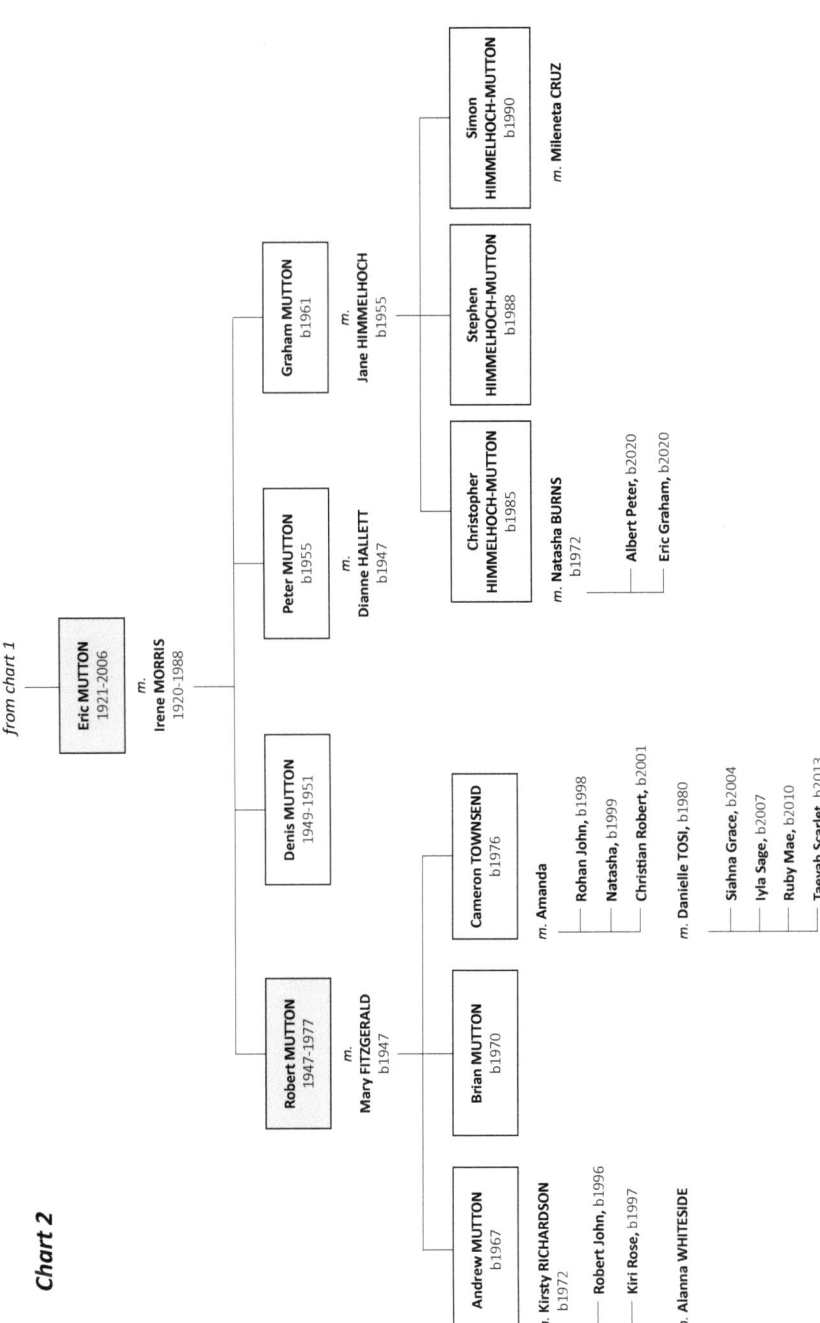

have originated from Mitten, meaning 'farmstead where two rivers join', the name can be found in the 1086 Domesday Book, albeit spelled Mitune. An early record of the family was Alan and Jordan de Mitton, who appeared in the Assize Rolls of Yorkshire in 1219.

Despite available online resources, thorough research of ancestors more than 250 years ago demands considerable time and expense. Often, confirming a probable link requires the purchase of documentary evidence not available via the Internet. In any case, this book is about Bob, not the entire family, so this short exposé will suffice. In addition, over 400 entries are now recorded, and presenting a complete family tree in a book the size of this one is impractical. What follows is a sectional graphic view of Bob's family story, as far back as his g-g-g-grandfather, Samuel, born in 1773. Also presented are his many grandchildren, none of whom, sadly, he ever met.

It is perhaps worth recording here that Bob was the second of 12 consecutive male births in the Mutton family, starting with Eric, who had four sons. Bob had three sons, as did Graham. With Eric born in 1921, it was a long wait, till 1997, before the tree saw a new feminine name.

◆

The Mutton coat of arms or family crest, 1195.

2. Bob's Story

England

Bob was born on Sunday, 5 January 1947, in Gosport, Hampshire, England. His parents were Eric and Irene[3] Mutton, who married in February 1945. Bob's given names, Robert John, are presumed to have been in honour of his paternal grandfather, John Frederick[4], and paternal great-grandfather, Robert[5]. His four grandparents died between 1949 and 1952, so any memories of them would have been slight. Neither Graham nor Peter recall Bob ever mentioning them.

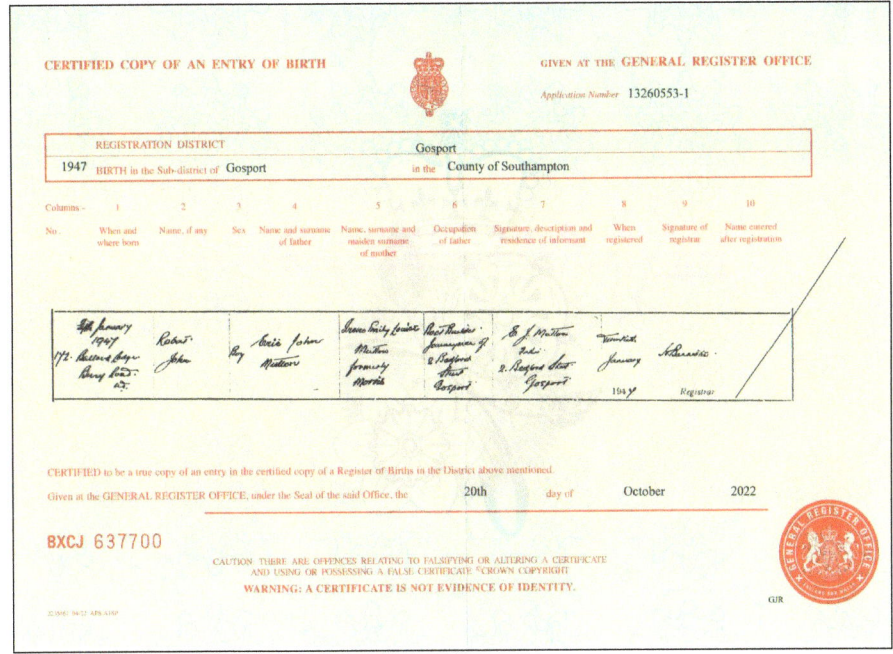

Bob's birth certicate.

---

3   Irene was usually known as Rene; later references to her use this shortened name.
4   John Frederick Mutton (1874 – 1951), Bob's paternal grandfather.
5   Robert Mutton (c1836 – 1881), Bob's paternal great-grandfather.

Only two photos of Bob survive that can be dated to 1947.

Eric with Bob on the waterfront, Portsmouth, 1947.

Robert Morris (son of Arthur and Eva Morris) and Bob, 1947.

Eric's first mention of Bob in his memoirs[6] reads, 'We were happy, and in 1947 Robert John (Bob) was born with Denis James a year or so later. But all the time, like many other returned servicemen, I couldn't settle. I'd get very depressed. My mother's illness was also a burden; she died of cancer soon after Denis was born in 1949.' Again, Bob is not known to have discussed Denis, who died tragically in 1951 when Bob was 4½ years old. Eric and Rene, in their grief, seemed to have suppressed their memories of Denis, which may have affected Bob's recollections of his younger brother.

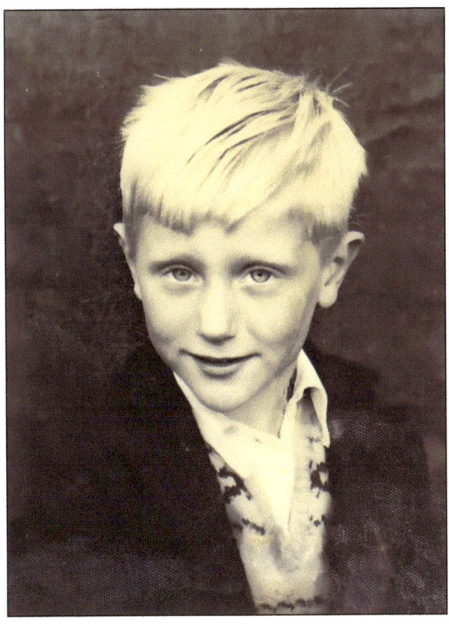

Bob, c1951

At the suggestion of Rene's doctor, the family opted for a change of environment and moved to Harwich, in Essex. Eric recalled, 'All that time, Bobby... only four years old, was bewildered, to say the least, but soon settled down and happily started school.'

Two years later, the coast of Essex was subject to significant flooding. This was caused by a severe storm over the North Sea, combined with a high spring tide. It affected coastal areas of England, Scotland, Belgium, and the Netherlands. On that night of 31 January / 1 February 1953, some 2,551 people lost their lives. In addition, over 47,000 buildings were damaged. One of those buildings was number 17 Victoria Street, Dovercourt, the home of Eric, Rene and Bob Mutton.

Eric recorded:

'... Rene and I stood shivering at the top of the stairs viewing with dismay our treasured possessions floating around in that filthy water. There was not much we could do, but at least we could keep warm upstairs and have

---

6 *The Spice of Life – Centenary Edition*, ISBN 978-0-6487713-3-3

something to eat. Young Bob, just turned six, thought it a great adventure. My main concern was for him and Rene. Obviously, it was best that they go to stay with her family in London.'

Bob spent three weeks in London with his mother. No doubt both were comforted and well looked after by Rene's family, but later in February, they returned to Harwich. Their home was then dry and warm though it took a lot of maintenance to return it to its pre-flood condition. Eric was able to

Harwich flooded, 1953

undertake much of this restoration work himself, ably assisted by finance provided by flood relief organisations.

Bob was well settled into a Harwich school by this time. Unfortunately, we have no record of which one he attended, but we have a photo taken at the school. It shows a 'cheeky chappie' seemingly quite happy being photographed.

In June 1955, Eric and Rene had another son, Peter David. Bob had a younger brother though the earliest photo of the pair suggests that he wasn't particularly impressed with the new addition to the family. Eric and Rene secured a few more photos of Bob in 1957.

The year proved to be a watershed one with the decision to emigrate to Australia. Eric and Rene, born in 1921 and 1920, were of the age to have known the 1930s depression, World War 2 and the 1953 North Sea Flood. Added to this, the loss of Denis in 1951 must have led to serious thinking about the future. Australia's Assisted Passage Migration Scheme, introduced in 1945, was in full swing and popular with British subjects. For a modest £10[7] ($20) per adult – children travelled free – every year, thousands of Ten Pound Poms made their way to Australia.

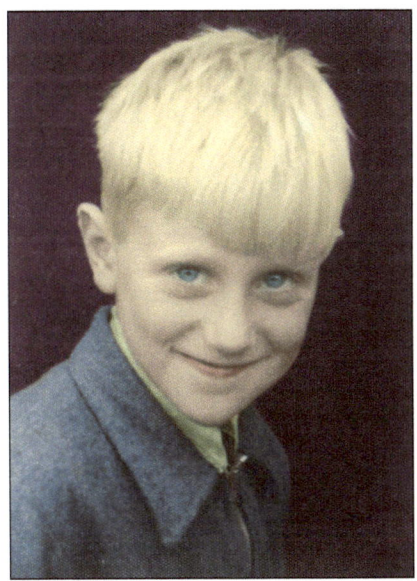
Bob, a school photo, 1953.

Eric and Rene were interviewed at Australia House in London and were delighted when advised that their application had been approved. It was to be many months, however, before the big move. Bob turned 11 in January 1958, perhaps old enough to realise the enormity of the impending change to his life. But, curiously, he never discussed any aspects of his early life with Peter or Graham. Herein lies an odd aspect of Bob's relationship with his surviving brothers. Being eight years older than Peter and 14 years senior to Graham, the three siblings didn't experience the brotherly association typically enjoyed by other families.

How Bob emotionally processed his departure from 'home' is impossible to determine. Even at the tender age of 11½, permanently leaving familiar surroundings and friends must have been a wrench. Nevertheless, with his parents and young brother Peter – aged three and oblivious of what was going on – on 26 June 1958, he boarded TV *Fairsky*[8] at Southampton. The

---

7   £10 in 1958 was the equivalent of about £180 ($A310) in 2022.
8   The 26 June 1958 sailing was the maiden voyage of Sitmar Line's TV *Fairsky* as a passenger vessel. Laid down as SS *Steel Artisan* in 1941, the ship was incarnated as USS *Barnes* (1942), HMS *Attacker* (1942–1945), and *Castel Forte* (1950–1958) before being fitted out specifically for the Britain to Australia Assisted Passage Migration Scheme.

Bob with younger brother Peter, 1955 or 1956.

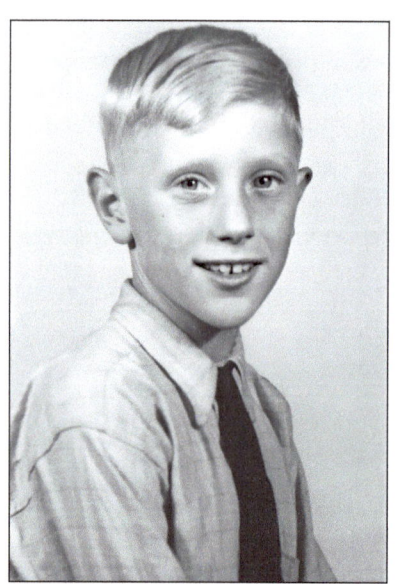

Bob, studio portrait, 1957.

Bob, school photo, 1957.

manifest of the voyage records that the Mutton family were four of 1,481 passengers on board, of which 1,430 were braving emigration to far-off Australia. Their address is listed as "La Tour", Knockholt Pound, Knockholt, Kent. Presumably, this was a temporary residence between the sale of Eric and Rene's Harwich house and their departure for Australia.

Eric recorded his thoughts on leaving home[9]:

Bob with Peter, 1957.

'Sailing from Southampton on a fine, sunny summer evening, Rene and I stood on deck, seeing, perhaps for the last time, the familiar sights of Hampshire, our former hometown Gosport, and the oh-so-familiar entrance to Portsmouth Harbour. To starboard my favourite pre-war playground, the Isle of Wight. It brought a lump to my throat. "What have we let ourselves in for?" I said. No reply. I guess she felt as I did.

'That feeling soon passed when we quickly made friends with those who shared our table at dinner that night and for the rest of the voyage. Later we entered the Bay of Biscay, which was living up to its reputation, very rough. Rene was seasick and took to her bunk, where she stayed right through Biscay and the Mediterranean until we docked at Port Said. The skills of our steward, even the ship's doctor's attentions, were to no avail.

'Never having experienced sea sickness myself, caring for her, Bob, who was also sick for a day or two, and looking after three-year-old Peter was no problem. I was enjoying myself. Two of our dining room companions, both male, were seasick. Their wives were not, so for the first few days, I was companion to two ladies and their children.'

Peter recalls Eric saying that one day he advised Bob to go forward for some fresh air during a spate of seasickness. As well as fresh air, he enjoyed a drenching from an unsympathetic rogue wave

---

9   *The Spice of Life – Centenary Edition*, ISBN 978-0-6487713-3-3

Bob – The Short Life of Robert John Mutton

TV *Fairsky*, a Sitmar Line postcard, c1958.

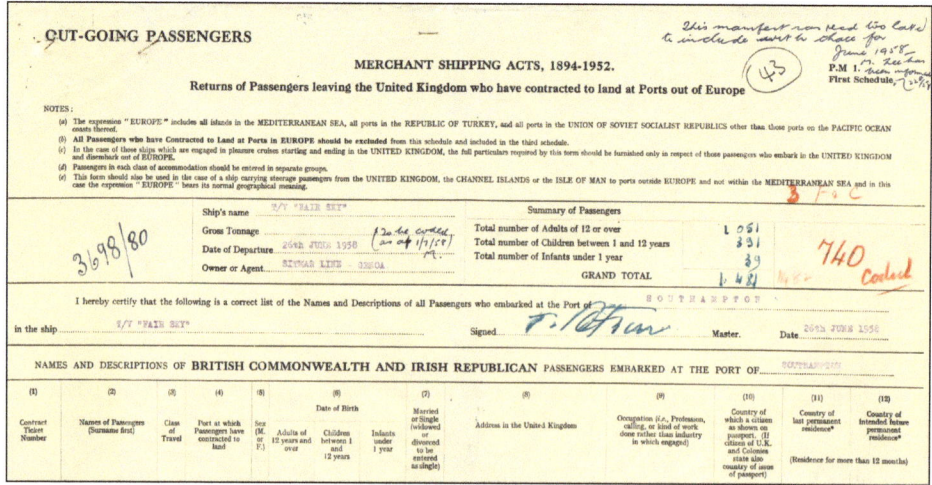

Section of the *Fairsky* passenger manifest, 26 June 1958.

No.	NAME.		CLASS.	PORT OF EMBARKATION.	PORT OF INTENDED DEBARKATION.	ADDRESS AT DESTINATION IN AUSTRALIA.*
564	MUTTON	ERIC J.	DO	SOUTHAPTON	MELBOURNE	117 NEWTOWN RD. HOBART TASMANIA
565	MUTTON	IRENE	DO	DO	DO	DO
566	MUTTON	ROBERT	DO	DO	DO	DO
567	MUTTON	PETER	DO	DO	DO	DO

Extract from the Australian Department of Health Quarantine Service Passenger List.

breaking over the bow. No doubt, the seasickness was momentarily forgotten.

Fairsky docked at Fremantle, Western Australia, on 21 July, where Eric, Rene and their two sons took a local train and spent a few hours seeing the sights of Perth. A few days later, the ship arrived in Melbourne. Eric recorded, 'A quick flight across Bass Strait brought us to Hobart on a cold, wet winter evening on Saturday, 26 July 1958, exactly one month after leaving England.' The 117 New Town Road 'Address at Destination' was a comfortable hostel, ideal short-term accommodation for weary travellers or immigrants. It is now a Salvation Army facility.

◆

M	"La Tour", Knockholt Pound, Knockholt, Kent.	Shipwright/Boat Builder	25
M	do	Wife	
S	do	Son	✓
S	do	Son	

Bob's crossing the equator certificate from King Neptune ('the best, the greatest, the truest god of the seas'), 12 July 1958.

3. Bob's Story

Australia, Hobart and Launceston

It's winter 1958, and Eric and Rene decided to rent a cottage at Fern Tree, leaving their short-term hostel accommodation in New Town. An outlying suburb of Hobart, Fern Tree is conveniently only 9km from the city. However, in the foothills of Mount Wellington and at an elevation of 400 metres, the colder months can be bitter. This accommodation proved short-lived when Rene decided she didn't leave cold England simply to live in a different cold environment.

Lenah Valley was the family's next chosen suburb. An arrangement was made with one Doug Southwood of 33 Toorak Avenue, whereby we secured free (or cheap) accommodation in exchange for housekeeping services. Of course, this was Rene's domain, though Eric looked after the garden. Bob's bedroom was at the front of the house, while Peter made do with the sunroom, accessed through that front bedroom.

Bob secured a job when we were at Lenah Valley, becoming a part-time paperboy. Newsagents engaged young lads to sell the *Saturday Evening Mercury* door to door. I understand our local newsagent was something of a tyrant who didn't allow his boys to keep their tips, claiming they were actually intended for him. His idea of a fair day's pay – all of two shillings (20 cents) – for a fair day's work wasn't Bob's idea, and he didn't stay a paperboy for very long.

Bob's schooling continued, of course, though it's not recorded where he completed his primary school education. He attended Hobart High School[10] at Letitia Street, North Hobart. High school education continued till 1962 when he earned his Schools Board Certificate. Despite a rather underwhelming result, it appeared not to hinder his employment and advancement.

---

10 Hobart High School opened in 1903 and became the Hobart High Matriculation College in 1965. The name changed to Hobart Matriculation College in 1967 and abbreviated to Hobart College in 1987.

Schools Board of Tasmania

Schools Board Certificate

Nº xxx36235x
Duplicate.

This is to Certify that ROBERT JOHN MUTTON has completed a four-year course of general education approved by the Schools Board of Tasmania, and has in compliance with its by-laws obtained the results listed below.

Subject	Result	Points	Year of passing
English II	P	2	1962
Science IIA (Physics)	L	1	1962
Mathematics II	P	2	1962
French I	P	1	1962

Total points 6

This is to certify that the abovenamed candidate has qualified for the endorsement marked "Qualified" below:

Qualified or Not Qualified

ENDORSEMENT A:
The candidate has complied with the provisions of the by-laws requiring the prescribed qualification on basic subjects.

NOT QUALIFIED

ENDORSEMENT B:
The candidate has gained not less than seven points, but has not qualified for Endorsement A.

NOT QUALIFIED

Signed on behalf of the Schools Board of Tasmania.
Date 15th May, 1973.

Chairman

This certificate is issued without any alterations.
(For explanation see back hereof)

Bob's Schools Board Certificate, 1962.

Hobart High School, as it would have appeared when Bob was a pupil there from 1959 to 1962.
Source: Ash, Bester's postcard, 1950s.

During these early years in Hobart, Eric joined the British Ex-Service League and Royal Automobile Club of Tasmania. According to Eric, friends were soon made at various social functions, 'mostly in our own age group and British migrants, all facing the same settling-in problems[11].' Those friends included John (Jack) and Gladys (Queenie) Fitzgerald. Their elder daughter, Mary, met Bob in 1961. More about that later.

Eric started his Hobart working life on the waterfront, and after a couple of years, he successfully applied for the position of Shipwright Surveyor with the Marine Board of Hobart. Tenancy of a Marine Board house at Battery Point came with the job, and taking up the option, the family moved into number 2, Battery Square, in 1961. Everyone loved that house, as it had large rooms, and Eric was able to utilise one of the bedrooms as a workshop.

Peter documented his memories:

'To the west side of the house, on its own little block of land, was a semaphore mast. This was no longer in use, of course, by the time we moved there, telegraphy and telephones long having made it obsolete. It wasn't quite useless though. When Bob became interested in radio, he used the mast to gain considerable height for a long-wire antenna. Being

---

11 *The Spice of Life – Centenary Edition*, ISBN 978-0-6487713-3-3

on slightly elevated ground already, the added height would have provided much-improved reception.

'Next to my room was the sunroom where Bob and I, with others roped in, would spend hours playing Monopoly, Chinese checkers, draughts and other board games. Park And Shop was another favourite, a game I haven't seen around for many years, except on eBay[12].'

Some of these board games were based more on luck than skill, so the age difference was largely irrelevant, and the older brother didn't always win.

Bob had enjoyed stamp collecting for some years and, also in 1961, introduced the joys of that hobby to Peter. He collected stamps of the whole world, as did most young collectors, but his album was strongest in Great Britain and Australia. Eric and Rene frequently corresponded with their many siblings in England, and Bob was the benefactor of the British stamps that arrived on return letters. Young people of today can hardly

2 Battery Square (single-storey red brick house with pitched roof), Battery Point, showing the semaphore mast in situ, 1960. This is a view from Lenna Hotel, the vista downriver now spoiled by the 12-storey Empress Towers.

---

12 *Twenty Five Years*, ISBN 978-0-9873470-5-3

comprehend the volume of communication that went through the postal service in the early 1960s.

Bob had enjoyed stamp collecting for some years and, also in 1961, introduced the joys of that hobby to Peter. He collected stamps of the whole world, as did most young collectors, but his album was strongest in Great Britain and Australia. Eric and Rene frequently corresponded with their many siblings in England, and Bob was the benefactor of the British stamps that arrived on return letters. Young people of today can hardly comprehend the amount of communication that went through the postal service in the early 1960s.

Much occurred about this time, and in 1961, at age 14, Bob was diagnosed with diabetes. He had been unwell for some time, and the diagnosing doctor was surprised his condition hadn't already been recognised. This must have been mid-year, during the colder months, as Peter remembers Bob spending time in bed enjoying the comfort of a kerosene heater. The family otherwise didn't heat rooms other than the lounge:

> 'It must have been winter, as I recall him in bed, with a kerosene heater warming the room. One day he was listening to music on an open reel tape recorder, also called reel-to-reel. He asked me to turn up the heater. Being unfamiliar with the device, I turned it up too high, and it flared alarmingly. I was sure I was going to burn the house down and was too frightened to touch it again. Bob had to climb out of bed and rectify the situation. I was never quite comfortable with kerosene heaters after that.'

Bob's choice of music may have been typical of the times, and his preferences influenced Peter and Graham, young as they were. He was keen on Gene Pitney, the Everly Brothers, and later the Beatles. He also bought the James Bond *Goldfinger* soundtrack LP record.

On a happier note, there was much excitement in the household when Eric's nephew Kevin Fuge visited later in the year. Kevin was the son of Reg and Win Fuge, Win being one of Eric's sisters. Kevin had chosen a maritime career and, as a 16-year-old midshipman, visited Hobart aboard (appropriately) the *Port Hobart*.

This was Kevin's first trip to sea. He left Liverpool mid-September, calling in at Aden, Fremantle, Adelaide, Melbourne, and then Hobart. Kevin estimates his visit would have been in October or November 1961. Happily, the solitary photograph recording the event was of him and Bob in the garden of 2 Battery Square. Kevin later claimed that he always put our address in pencil in his records because it changed so often.

Bob, with cousin Kevin who visited briefly when his ship *Port Hobart* called into Hobart in late 1961.

An even happier event occurred on 13 October 1961 with the birth of Graham Roy. Bob promptly gave him the nickname Grum, which seems to have stuck, at least as far as Peter is concerned. Bob also called Peter Egbert, Charlie or Sam for no apparent reason, although only Sam found long-term favour.

Saturday nights at Battery Point were something out of the ordinary for Bob and Peter. They were tasked with walking to the nearest newsagent to buy the *Saturday Evening Mercury*, otherwise known as the SEM. The newsagent on Morrison Street, near the docks, was only a 10-minute walk through Princes Park and along Salamanca Place. Thus, Bob's abortive experience as a paperboy in Lenah Valley was reborn. Peter recalls some bribery involved, and sweets were purchased along with the newspaper.

Bob finished his schooling in 1962 and took a job at Bankers & Traders Insurance[13]. Their offices were in the city and easily within walking distance. As a matter of family (in)significance, the entity was formally registered

---

13 Bankers & Traders Insurance Company Limited was taken over by QBT Holdings Limited in 1973, now called QBE Insurance Group Limited.

just six weeks before Eric was born. A benefit of Bob's job was that some days he would bring Peter an envelope full of stamps that he'd managed to salvage from the office mail. Peter was particularly impressed with the higher denominations he could add to his growing collection.

Bob's interest in radio continued, and his first foray into competition occurred in August 1963. Using an AWA 3BZ receiver, he accumulated 424 points in the 1963 RD Contest. Graham surmises that his receiver 'must have been already in the house at Battery Square when we moved in. This is probably not an unreasonable piece of guesswork given that these radios were used by the coast watch service and the house belonged to the Port of Hobart, plus its connection with Mount Nelson Signal Station. Bob was also unlikely to have been able to buy such a set at that time.'

Graham has since bought an example of the 3BZ and had it expertly restored. He conjectures that his particular set may have been Bob's actual receiver. It's unlikely, but you never know.

Graham's restored AWA 3BZ receiver, the same model Bob used in his early years as a radio enthusiast.

Along with stamp collecting and radio, Bob toyed with other hobbies. Peter remembers his older brother building model locomotives, carriages and other rolling stock. Even today, the smell of a particular glue brings back memories of those innocent times. A brief flirtation with painting resulted in a rendering of a Parisian street scene with, inevitably, the Eiffel Tower in the background. While only a colour-by-numbers effort and rather gaudily presented, it holds a certain fascination and naive charm. Graham has the original, and Peter intends to have a print of it framed.

Bob's only known effort at painting, a Parisian street scene.

Photos of the family in the early days are scarce and much treasured. Eric had a Kodak 'Brownie' 127 camera, possibly brought out from England but more likely purchased in Hobart. The oldest surviving photo is the one of Bob and Kevin, but another happily extant image is one of Bob, Graham and Peter taken on Christmas Day, 1963. This was taken at Battery Square and shows the boys sitting on the back step of the house. Peter proudly displays a toy glider that provided some fun until Bob accidentally trod on it, ending its flying days. This is the only known photo of the three brothers together.

1964 rolled around, and we moved into number 33, Hampden Road, still in Battery Point and only a few minutes' walk from Battery Square.

Bob, Graham and Peter, Christmas Day 1963.

Eric and Rene had taken over the proprietorship of a small general store on the corner of Runnymede Street. Born of opportunity rather than strategy, the family now lived above its shop, though (as the saying goes) not beyond its means. Peter and Graham still refer to this period of their lives as when they 'had the shop.'

Of the previous owners, we know nothing other than Mr R. Ketchell was a stamp collector. We discovered this only recently when Peter spotted a 1962 first day cover for sale on eBay. This was eagerly purchased and is the earliest surviving envelope addressed to one of our homes.

While at Hampden Road, Bob secured his driving licence and bought a car. Licencing conventions were more straightforward in the early sixties, and, no doubt, his driving tuition was Eric's task.

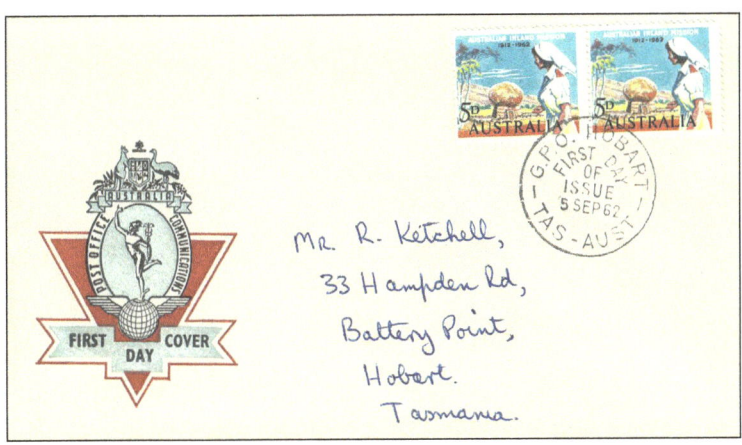

A first day cover of 1962 addressed to one of the previous owners of 'the shop'.

Peter recorded:

> 'It was an FJ Holden, now known affectionately as a humpy due to the bulging bonnet. My big brother was growing up. I think it was originally white but Bob repainted it black using dozens of cans of spray paint. At the time, it looked pretty good, but I now doubt the amateur respray was of the highest quality. In the meantime, Dad drove a Volkswagen beetle (replacing a 1939 Hillman).'[14]

Graham remembered:

> 'It reminds me that Dad once said Bob used to run errands for them after he got his licence when we had the shop in Hampden Road. Assuming licence conditions were much the same as now, he must have got his licence as soon as he turned 17 or very shortly thereafter. Anyway, I remember Dad saying how Bob had a bit of a crash on one of these errands and had "200 eggs" sitting on the back seat, all of which were smashed and made a "hell of a mess".'

Bob and his FJ Holden, with friend Steven Wright, c1965.
Steve Wright and a friend, Colin West, were involved in a car accident. Tragically, Steve was killed immediately, with no visible injuries except a bruise on his temple. Mary was nursing at the time. She recalls it was a huge shock as she lived opposite two nurses who went out with Colin at different times. She thinks one was his girlfriend at the time.

Peter clearly remembers the family sitting 'in the front room' (in reality, at the side of the house) watching newsreel footage (on black-and-white TV) of the 1964 Tokyo Olympic Games. This was in October when Graham turned three and would have been too young to care.

---

14 *Twenty Five Years*, ISBN 978-0-9873470-5-3

Bob's life took a turn when the family lived at Hampden Road. As mentioned already, Eric and Rene became friends with Jack and Queenie Fitzgerald soon after arriving in Hobart. Their elder daughter, Mary, remembers Bob in those early days:

> 'I didn't think of or have much to do with him until I was about 16. John[15] was his friend. I had a sleepover with a friend (last year of school) and decided to go to a disco. We caught a bus to the city or North Hobart (not sure), and to my surprise, Bob and his friend boarded the bus and sat in front of us. Of course, a conversation ensued: where, what, going there? May we join you? We agreed, and I remember that we had a great night.
>
> 'A couple of weeks later, we met up again to go roller skating at Moonah. Bob was hopeless, but then I could not ride a bike. Drinks in those days were milkshakes and sodas; neither of us drank alcohol, being under 21. Unfortunately, our friends went their separate ways. We met up a couple of times, and then it was time for me to study for final exams. He was working at Bankers & Traders.
>
> 'I commenced nursing, and as I lived quite a distance from home, transport was a problem. Rene suggested that I have meals with the family if I could not get home/back to the hospital on days off etc. I didn't miss not going home too much. It worked quite satisfactorily, and Bob was persuaded (apparently not too much persuasion on his part. I was still very

Bob (front row, left) with fellow staff members of Bankers & Traders, c1966.

---

15   John Fitzgerald, Mary's brother.

shy) to drive me to and from the hospital/home. We became great friends and started our relationship as a couple.

'We had fun times together, having a similar sense of humour; his was more wicked than mine. He loved to drive. After a hospital dance (curfew 10.30), along with another couple, we decided to travel to Mount Wellington. Lots of laughter and freezing cold; halfway up, we turned around and arrived back very late (early). Wearing long frocks and high heels, the boys gave us a leg up over the high Nursing Home shut gates. Giggling, with one shoe lost, we finally snuck up to our rooms. Amazingly, we were not caught. Bob would not return my shoe – 'No. Cinderella has lost her shoe.' To this day, I do not know what happened to it. I think the heel snapped off.

'His special name for me was Squirt; 'my darling, beautiful, loving Squirt.'

Peter remembers that at about this time, Bob bought a block of land at Blackman's Bay, a suburb about 15km south of the city. He thinks it cost £500 ($1000), but this may be incorrect.

As with many of the family's accommodations, being 'at the shop' didn't last long, and another move was made. Eric recorded:

'In almost two years, we had lived well and had saved enough to put down a healthy deposit on the purchase of a house. When we decided that it was time to relax a bit, we quickly found a buyer for the business. A young couple, like us, recent migrants with a growing family. He was gainfully employed and, like me, had a wish to be able to supplement his income. We agreed on the price and a takeover date, bought a house in Moonah, then an outer suburb of Hobart, and with relief, settled down to a quieter life.'[16]

The first of several forays to Hobart's northern suburbs saw the Mutton family at 24 Springfield Avenue, Moonah, in 1965. Bob and Mary were very much 'an item' by now. Peter remembers the day they announced their engagement to Eric and Rene.

Mary remembers one rocky episode during their early romance days:

'... one night, he drove me home, and we had an argument. I was very annoyed as I got out of the car to walk home. We were not too far from my house. Unknown to me, Bob followed me to check that I was fine. Dad said to me, "Where's Bob? I didn't hear the car." I went to my bedroom; I do not think I answered him. Apparently, he went to the window and saw Bob. Both waved, and he knew I was in safe hands.'

---

16 *The Spice of Life – Centenary Edition*, ISBN 978-0-6487713-3-3

Their wedding was at St Mary's Cathedral, in Hobart, on Saturday, 12 November 1966. It was a typically unseasonal Hobart day, but rain failed to dampen the joy of the occasion. Thus, Bob became the first in his line of the Mutton family to be married in Australia eight years after arriving in the country. Neither Peter nor Graham remembers much of the event.

l-r: [?], Peter, Rene, Bob (holding Graham's hand), Mary, Ann Fitzgerald, Jack Fitzgerald (behind Ann), Queenie Fitzgerald, John Fitzgerald.

Eric's sister Mabs visited soon after the 7 February 1967 bushfires. After nine years in Australia, Mabs was the first in-person meeting with one of the many relatives we had left behind. It was a joyful reunion. Bob would have remembered her from 'the old days'.

Another happy event of 1967 was the birth of Bob and Mary's first son, Andrew. By November – possibly earlier – they were residents of New Town, having rented a flat in Roope Street. This proved to be short-term accommodation, though, as by December 1967, they had moved to Jordan Hill Road in West Hobart, a little closer to the city but further away from Bob's parents in Moonah. At about this time, Mary's parents, Jack and Queenie Fitzgerald moved to Sydney.

Cutting the cake.

With Mary's sister, Ann.

Rene, Eric, Ann, Bob and Mary.

Bob with Andrew in the garden of the Fitzgerald family home, Pottery Road, Lenah Valley, 1967.

Mary and Bob with Andrew, one of his earliest photos, appropriately sitting on a car, 1967.

Mary recalled an incident when Andrew at 14 months old:

> '… was attacked by a plover at Sandy Bay Beach. With arms windmilling, Bob rushed to rescue him and his little trolley. Like a weightlifter, he snapped up both trolley and child, almost slipping over. It now seems funny, but it wasn't at the time. If I remember correctly, we were having a picnic with you all. At the time of Bob's death, the two of them were beginning to bond – Dad and his eldest son.'

Mary and Bob at Nutgrove Beach, Sandy Bay, the venue of the incident with the plover.

In 1968, Bob, Mary and Andrew suffered a car accident. Mary recorded the experience:

> 'We were driving north to visit our friends Jill (Andrew's godmother) and Robert in Burnie. We travelled via Cradle Mountain National Park, as I had never been there. It seemed like good weather – in those days there were no weather details at our fingertips – but unfortunately, typical Tassie, the rain turned into sleet and then snow.
>
> 'We were driving through Hellyer Gorge, slowly crossing an old rutted wooden bridge. The front wheels left the wood, and the car skidded. We ended up hitting a very small tree trunk, enough to write off the car. Andrew (18 months old) was asleep in the back, and there wasn't a mark on him. Both Bob and I had similar facial injuries, but as he was a diabetic, they were very concerned. However, I had problems with glass fragments embedded in my skull, which finally emerged with no problems.'

Bob also provided a brief report in his amateur radio column in ADXN, where he thanked members:

> '... who expressed their sympathy etc to myself and my family. For those who did not know, we were involved in a car accident on the 31st of March and held in hospital for a week, 200 miles from home. Anyway, that is over. I'm left with a 5" scar just above my eyes.'

Mary also remembers that they sold their block of land at Blackman's Bay shortly after the accident. Unfortunately, it is not recorded whether the accident influenced that decision. Coincidentally, and vaguely related, Peter remembers Bob and Mary seemingly taking an interest in motor racing in 1968:

> '... Bob and Mary took me to watch the stock car racing. My brother and his wife must not have had a car of their own at the time, as they borrowed Dad's work van. Naturally, I had to sit rather uncomfortably in the back. This was before seatbelts were compulsory elements of modern life, so it was quite legal, though clearly less than satisfactory from a safety perspective.
>
> 'I clearly recall two such trips, though there may have been more. The first was memorable for the weather. It must have been the height of summer, as the day was dry and hot. In those days, you could park your car around the track and watch from the comfort of your own vehicle. In our case, Bob parked back-in, and we sat on the floor of the van, presumably on some cushioning material. On the day in question, each time the racing cars headed in our direction, we had to momentarily close the back doors to prevent the van filling with clouds of dust.'

Graham remembers car trips:

> 'Bob always loved going for drives and would take us/me to see odd transmitter sites on hilltops in weird places. He also took me to soccer games, at least once at Grove Road.'

As mentioned earlier, Bob took a job with Bankers & Traders Insurance soon after completing his high school education. He was in the industry for some time, as Mary reports:

> 'He worked hard to improve himself. He was very good with numbers and like all of you and my boys, curious and interested in life and all sorts of trivia. He worked in the Insurance industry for several years; exams for Fire, Accident, Marine and Life were required to succeed. I can't remember the name of the second company he worked for. He was transferred from the Hobart office to Launceston, where, as manager, he opened up the north and midlands area for the company. A takeover of the company occurred, and he was sent to Hobart to manage this office as his boss became CEO of Tasmania.
>
> 'I stayed in Launceston with the children, not working but being a stay-at-home Mum. He was once again working away from home, except he was away all week this time, not a couple of nights. No suitable rental was available. He arrived home unexpectedly one day as he had resigned. He was not happy with the changes being made within the company. We bought a shop which was a failure. Meanwhile, I returned to nursing.
>
> 'John lived with us in Launceston after he left school. He missed his mates and his band. We would go and watch them play. Andrew was

Bob happily ensconced in his Launceston home, 1969.

The radio corner.

The Launceston Rovers team with Bob third from right, back row, 1969/70.

their biggest fan. Much to my disgust, the band, including Bob, would go camping, 'roo shooting'. As far as I know, they never harmed any fauna. The only time was when a kangaroo was hit by a car. John enjoyed his time with us but soon realised he had to grow up. We both missed having him around, a wonderful babysitter. Both boys loved their Uncle John when he visited several times.'

The family home in Launceston was on Barton Street, Mowbray. While in Launceston, Bob took up (or returned to) soccer and played for Launceston Rovers as fullback. He was a strong player and a valuable member of the team. Also involved in the club's administration; he was the club treasurer for a time. One year, Andrew and Brian were the club mascots. Sadly, no photo has survived.

Andrew remembers:

'... watching Dad play football, and I do recall standing behind the goals, especially as he played fullback. I don't remember watching games outside of that, but I recall a time I played table tennis in what I can only assume were the clubrooms. There was another kid about the same age as me, and I think his name was Chris, and the table was so high that I could barely see over it, and the net was so far away.'

In March 1970, Bob and Mary welcomed their second son, Brian, who records his earliest memory of:

Bob, with Andrew and Brian, Launceston, 1970 or 1971.

'... being on the hill at (I think) Symmons Plains raceway. Mum has always said that I was only two and that my memory of this is because someone told me about it, but I can picture it in my head, so...'

The interest in motor racing clearly continued after Brian was born, as Mary recalls:

'Matchbox cars were very important; the boys always had one in their pockets, and so did Daddy. Car racing was a special occasion. Brian was always affected by the noise, always on Dad's shoulders. One day at Symmons Plains raceway, we were seated on a slight hill. Next minute, the pram decided to join the cars on the racetrack. The brake had failed to connect properly. Andrew never knew how close he came to driving in a car race fast asleep. I was eventually banned for plane and train spotting, much to my delight. It was boys-only time.

Eric, Mary, Andrew, Brian, Bob, Rene and Peter.
A family gathering at Elwick Road, Glenorchy, 1972.

A family picnic day at Mount Field National Park, 1973

Bob and Brian.

Graham, Mary, Andrew, Rene, Eric, Brian and Bob.

Rene, Mary, Andrew, Eric, Bob, Brian, and (in front) Peter.

'I lived with ham radio, cars, planes and trains. Andrew was always fascinated by Bob's radio and would sit on his knee and play with his cards. I would knit, read, sew or watch TV when the world "signed on".'

Mary relates an amusing story:

'... about Brian. Bob came home from afternoon/evening shift very tired, but it was his turn to check on the boys during the night. I heard Brian get up and nudge Bob to check on him. I rolled over he mumbled he's OK. The next morning getting dressed, he went to his sock drawer, and there were some very damp socks. Brian, instead of going to the bathroom, ended up in our bedroom and, being half asleep, mistook the open drawer for the toilet. After that, Bob did his duty just in case it occurred again, which it didn't, although Brian had a time when he sleepwalked. Brian would follow his big brother and Dad as much as he could. He was his little helper.'

Visits to Hobart were frequent. A favourite summer-time haunt of the family was Mount Field National Park, about 70km north of Hobart. Several picnics were enjoyed there, often with family friends. The preferred location was at the camping ground by the River Tyenna, a peaceful and picturesque spot with timber shelters provided. One such visit, in 1973, included Bob, Mary, Andrew and Brian. Happily, some photos recorded the event.

While living in Launceston, life took an unpleasant turn. Bob was often away from home and family, doing a job he was beginning to hate. Loneliness set in – Mary thinks stress as well – and Bob turned to gambling. He wouldn't discuss it, probably due to embarrassment. Their apparently idyllic life turned into one of financial difficulties. Mary threatened to leave and take the children to Sydney.

She thinks this may have put the idea into his head, and in 1973 the family indeed moved to Sydney. Other than an occasional visit to the Wrest Point casino when visiting Hobart, Bob saw the light and the gambling ceased.

At this point in the story, it seems appropriate to relate that Bob's fascination with radio continued unabated. It appears to have been a fixed point in his psyche. Graham compiled a history of Bob's radio history which is presented here. The move must have necessitated some culling of possessions, as Peter ended up with his Trio 9R59DS receiver for the princely sum of $60. At this stage, Eric, Rene, Peter and Graham lived in Wyndham Road, Claremont, another northern suburb.

With no funds to buy anything, Graham was the recipient of a free record player. Bob had renovated a 'portable fold-up thingy'. It started Graham's fascination with music – 'I loved that unit' – which continues to this day. But, on the other hand, Peter couldn't maintain an interest in radio, and the Trio was onsold for the $60 he paid for it.

◆

AWA 3BZ receiver, manufactured from 1942.

4. Bob's DX History

- Aug 1963: Bob scores 424 points in the 1963 RD Contest. Is using an AWA 3BZ receiver at this time.
- Mar 1964: Bob scores 305 points in the 1964 John Moyle Field Day Contest.
- Aug 1964: Bob scores 308 points in the 1964 RD Contest. At this point, he takes up an interest in VHF radio as well, primarily logging aircraft plus amateur radio operators. What he uses for a receiver though is unknown.
- Aug 1965: Bob scores 671 points in the 1965 RD Contest. He has, by this time, joined the WIA as member L7031.
- Mar 1966: Bob scores 905 points in the 1966 John Moyle Field Day Contest, winning the Tasmania Receiving section.
- Apr 1966: Bob advertises in *Amateur Radio* magazine for various QSL addresses.
- May 1966: Bob reports in *Amateur Radio* magazine having received QSLs from VS6, CR9, ON4 and VK9.
- Jun 1966 (approx.): Bob joins the ARDXC as member #72.
- Jul 1966: Bob is reported in *Amateur Radio* magazine to have used the TRESS system (forerunner of the Telex) to send reception reports. Also reports receiving QSLs from ZK2AF, VR5AB, 7Q7PBD, EI3S, VK9XI, TG9AD and OD5BZ.
- Aug 1966: Bob scores 914 points in the 1966 RD Contest.
- Sep 1966: *Amateur Radio* magazine reports Bob having been listening mainly to 40m, and has QSLs from OK3UL and VP5RB.
- Jan 1967: *Amateur Radio* magazine reports Bob is now married and therefore 'quiet on the DX front'. Bob does, however, ask for QSL addresses for 9G1ND and VE3FJZ, giving his address as still being Springfield Avenue.
- Aug 1967: *Amateur Radio* magazine reports Bob has received QSLs from K8HUX, CR6CQ, UL7BG, JA1KHK, VK2AVA/LH and PY1NBF. He then has 81 confirmed countries heard.
- Nov 1967: Bob takes over editorship of the Amateur Radio section of ARDXC's newsletter *ADXN*. His address at the time is 2/30 Roope Street, New Town.

- Dec 1967: Bob's article 'Utility DXing (Part 1)... DXing Ships' appears in *ADXN*.
- Dec 1967: Bob's address is now 41 Jordan Hill Road, West Hobart.
- Mar 1968: Bob scores 515 points in the 1968 John Moyle Field Day Contest, winning the Tasmania Receiving section.
- Mar 1968: Bob and his family have a serious car accident in the north of Tasmania, landing him in hospital for a week and leaving him with a 5" scar above his eyes.
- Aug 1968: Bob scores 954 points in the 1968 RD Contest.
- Mar 1969: Bob reports in *ADXN* that he has '... at last managed to get onto 20mx with a new trannie using the old one as a BFO for SSB.' We know that the 'old one' is the AWA 3BZ, but what is the new one? It can't be the Trio 9R59DS, as that has its own BFO for SSB.
- May 1969: Bob reports his new address as 8 Barton Street, Mowbray, saying he has taken over the local branch of Bankers & Traders and is 'flat out'. Photos show his main receiver is still the 3BZ, but he has aircraft technical charts on the wall, so he still has a VHF receiver for aircraft.
- Jul 1969: Bob reports still being very busy but hopes to buy a new receiver soon, '... probably a Trio 9R59DE.'
- Aug 1969: Bob scores 1,318 points in the 1969 RD Contest, winning the Tasmania receiving section.
- Jan 1970: Bob completes his last *Amateur radio* section of *ADXN*.
- 1973: Bob and his family move to Sydney. He sells his Trio 9R59DS to Peter. We visit Xmas 1973.
- Nov 1975: Bob is now fully into VHF aircraft monitoring and CB radio (not yet legal, but widely used). He doesn't appear to have any form of shortwave receiver at this stage. Bob states his VHF log book has 6,731 entries and has taken 'just over' 11 years to do.
- Feb 1977: Bob purchases a Yaesu FRG-7 to get back into shortwave DX and as the first part of his amateur station. He states his intention to use the WIA correspondence course to study for his license. To purchase the FRG-7, he sells his Midland 893 CB radio but still owns a Realistic rig which is at that stage 'in for repair'.

Explanatory notes:

20m	The 20 metre amateur radio band, that is, the shortwave frequencies from 14 to 14.35 MHz.
3BZ	See AWA.

40m	The 40 metre amateur radio band, that is, the shortwave frequencies from 7 to 7.3 MHz.
ADXN	Australian DX News.
ARDXC	Australian Radio DX Club.
AWA	Amalgamated Wireless Australasia was Australia's most prominent radio-based electronics manufacturer of the 20th century. The 3BZ was a shortwave radio receiver manufactured from 1935 until 1940 and made famous during World War 2 for its use by Coastwatchers monitoring Japanese military movements in the Pacific.
BFO	Beat Frequency Oscillator. See SSB.
CB	Citizens Band radio. A once popular amateur two-way radio system based requiring no technical license.
DX	A radio term for 'distance' as in long-distance radio reception. DXing is the hobby of listening for and/or contacting radio stations over long distances.
John Moyle	See 'RD Contest'.
QSL	A postcard verifying contact with another radio station.
Midland	A popular manufacturer of CB radios in the 1970s and 1980s.
RD Contest	An annual contest conducted by the Wireless Institute of Australia in which amateur radio operators and shortwave listeners attempt to make as many contacts or hear as many amateur radio stations as possible in a set period. Same for John Moyle Field Day.
Realistic	A popular manufacturer/retailer of consumer electronics equipment.
Rig	Jargon for any form of radio transmitter.
SSB	Single Sideband – a form of narrow bandwidth radio communication commonly used by amateur radio operators on the shortwave bands. A BFO is used on specialised receivers to rectify these signals and make them intelligible.
Trio	An early name used by the Japanese Kenwood company manufacturing radio and other consumer electronics products. The 9R59DS was a popular shortwave communications receiver (radio) made in the 1960s and 1970s, with the 9R59DE its predecessor.
VHF	Very High Frequency. A part of the radio spectrum used for such things as FM radio and aircraft communications.
WIA	Wireless Institute of Australia. An organisation that looks after the interests of amateur radio operators and provides training courses for those wishing to sit for their amateur radio license.
Yaesu	A Japanese manufacturer of radio communications equipment. The FRG-7 was a very popular shortwave receiver from the 1970s.

◆

5. Bob's Story

Australia, Sydney

> Digression: The move to Sydney inevitably meant there was less day-to-day contact between Bob and his Hobart-based family. Peter and Graham stayed in touch by letter and, of course, there was always the telephone. The family visited Sydney for Christmas 1973. In that year, Graham turned 12 and Peter 18. The following narrative draws heavily on Mary's memories and those of Andrew and Brian.

On arrival in Sydney, Bob contacted Airlines of New South Wales[17] and, to his surprise, was offered a position. So started a new adventure. There were difficulties at first finding rental accommodation, and the family stayed with Mary's parents for a month or two. Andrew started school, and Mary, having left nursing due to continual pain, took a job as a stock clerk with Beaurepaires. A unit was finally found, though it was too small; they were used to a house and garden.

Later, presumably when space permitted, Bob and John Fitzgerald took on the restoration of a Volkswagen Kombi. Mary tells the story, describing the photo that follows:

> 'The two law-abiding citizens, very scruffy looking if caught by the police, I'd gaol them and throw away the key. John had a VW Kombi with a good engine, but the bodywork wasn't so good. On his way to work one day, Bob saw an abandoned Kombi under the Gladesville Bridge. Apparently, it had been there for some time. The two boys went to investigate. The engine was no good, but the bodywork was very good. No police markings anywhere, so they decided to tow it home one evening. The photo shows the idiot mechanics at work. John had that Kombi for years and travelled around Australia in it.
>
> 'Andrew, being Andrew, having been told not to try and climb on either Kombi, had to investigate, always curious. He cut open his leg and was rushed to hospital for stitches. Both John and Bob had a successful small business, constructing bunk beds. This ended when Bob died. John and Bob were great mates. They used to go bike riding together. John eventually told me he came to see me more than him, but I completely ignored him.'

---

17 Airlines of New South Wales was absorbed into Ansett Australia in 1993.

John Fitzgerald, Robyn and Bob 'rescuing' a VW Kombi, about 1974.

The bunk bed construction sideline was well-remembered, possibly because it took up so much time. It must have been a successful business, as Graham recalls:

'I do remember the bunk-building business he and John undertook, but don't recall ever seeing any of the product. Apparently, there was a huge demand for them, and they "flew out the (garage) door".'

In 1975 Bob and Mary, with the boys in tow, revisited Hobart for a welcome family reunion. Fortunately, several photos record the event, in particular, at Princes Park, Battery Point, above which sits the old family home at number 2, Battery Square.

Bob also flew down on his own that year and called in to see Peter in his 'crummy bed-sit flat' in Sandy Bay. Peter recorded in his own memoirs[18]:

'Bob was living now in Sydney, and we started a correspondence about things generally, and stamps specifically. He had a job as a booking clerk for the Airlines of New South Wales and was able to take cheap flights, albeit only on stand-by, which meant only when a seat was available. I think his occasional flights back to Hobart cost $10.

---

18 *Twenty-Five Years*, ISBN 978-0-9873470-5-3

'I remember one occasion when he paid a lightning visit to Hobart, and we took ourselves off to the Post Office Museum on Castray Esplanade. The museum has long since closed down, which is a great shame as it housed many fascinating exhibits. I wonder what became of the collection.'

On this occasion, and during other visits, Peter and Bob bought sheets of stamps at the museum's philatelic counter. These were for investment purposes. The stamps did appreciate in value, but they remained unsold, and the opportunity for profit was lost. Peter still has some of these stamps, but they are now worth less than face value.

Mary remembers some of their holiday adventures, camping:

'From an early age, the boys went camping. We travelled nearly all of Tasmania. He taught them so much, even though they probably don't realise or remember. Another memorable trip was when Andrew was about three. He was told to stay in the car, but, oh no, out he jumps and disappears in a snow drift. Bob literally pulled him out by the scruff of his neck, a very miserable little boy. We stopped to take a photo.

Bob usually drank 'dietetic beer' – typically Cascade's low carb D-Beer – but occasionally enjoyed a regular brew, 1975.

'Our last trip was to discover beyond the black stump. Bob bought an old Land Rover and made it mechanically sound with the help of Steve, his mechanic mate. Unfortunately, the rain was either in front or behind us. Roads became flooded from the recent seasonal river floods in the north. Do not cross flooded roads – "No", says Mary; "Yes", says Bob, after checking. It wasn't flowing, but halfway across, we became bogged. Luckily, a bulldozer was parked on the other side and came to our rescue.

'Bob was very chastened after a few words from the old feller. It was a lovely trip at the beginning. Bushwalking, sleeping under the stars; the boys in the Land Rover, we were outside, where you could seem to reach the stars. Seeing flora and fauna in their natural habitat, especially the huge span of the magnificent eagles, was a great experience for us all. I was nearly nine months pregnant with Cameron.'

Mary recalled that happy time in 1976 with the birth of Cameron:

'When Cameron was born, Bob took the three boys to his office. So I had a chance to spend a day on my own. Everyone wanted to know about the baby as he hadn't mentioned I was pregnant. How he kept it secret, I do not know!

'Cameron had this strange affinity with his dad. Every night (no kidding), when he arrived home from an afternoon or night shift, Cameron would wake up, and Bob would go to see him. I was in hospital with baby Cameron, waiting for his visit. I waited and waited. Finally, he arrived with bandaged fingers and hands, plus a tetanus shot. He had found an injured baby possum in the car park. Instead of alerting the reception staff, he tried to give it a helping hand. Thank goodness he didn't bring the other two. We do not know if the possum survived.

Mary, Bob, Graham, Rene and Eric, 1975.

Bob, Andrew, Mary taking an interest in the sundial at Princes Park, Battery Point, 1975. Brian (in front) isn't so interested.

Bob in his element, monitoring aeroplane radio transmissions at Hobart Airport, 1975.

Bob and Mary, 1975.

'From the time they were tiny at breakfast, he would sit them on his knee and read the paper to them. Daddy was always early morning stories, and Mummy was mostly bedtime stories. Unlike today, taking the boys out for a meal meant fish and chips etc. Depending on the weather, it was the park, along the river, at the beach or in the car. The two eldest competed with each other when their dad was around, especially as his job allowed him to be at home more than a traditional nine-to-five job. He made sure that they shared him equally and had his undivided attention. Sometimes I think I was left out.'

Despite a lessening of routine contact between the Sydney and Hobart families, visits appear to have been fairly regular. In 1976, Bob and Mary felt their first two sons were mature enough to travel to Hobart unaccompanied on an Ansett flight. Of course, they were met at the airport, two young boys happy to again be in the midst of their extended family.

At this time, the Mutton home was at Bridgewater, a suburb 22km north of Hobart and on the eastern side of the River Derwent. This address

Brian and Andrew at Hobart airport after their flight from Sydney, 1976.

proved advantageous as travel from the airport to Hobart on the western shore was curtailed by the Tasman Bridge disaster of January 1975. Andrew and Brian would probably not remember this event.

However, Brian confessed to:

> 'Vague recollections of climbing up the back fence at our grandparents' place (Bridgewater) to see the trains in the distance. We went to a salmon farm and the Cadbury factory with Eric. This was a trip Andrew and I made without our parents.'

Later in the year, Mary also visited to present baby Cameron to his grandparents. No doubt, Eric and Rene were delighted. The only photo that exists of this event was also taken at Hobart airport.

◆

Mary with Cameron visiting Hobart, 1976.

6. Of Planes, Radios and Automobiles

Graham:

'My memories of Bob are a little strange, being a mix of exotic places we would visit – or, I should say, places that seemed exotic to me as a young lad more than 14 years junior to Bob – and his strange but fascinating world of unusual hobbies and pastimes mixed with his infectious enthusiasm for everything and anything that captured his attention.

'In fact, my earliest memory of Bob isn't so much about Bob per se, but rather his hobbies, and in particular, shortwave radio. When I was two we moved house, and even at that tender age, such a jolt tends to stick in the mind. I have a clear delineation in my memory between the house I was born into and that of the few years from the age of two until I was about five.

'It has been mentioned elsewhere in this book that we surmise Bob took a keen interest in shortwave radio probably as a result of coming into possession of an AWA 3BZ Coastal Radio shortwave receiver. That was due to our fortuitous occupancy of the Assistant Harbour Master's house at Battery Square, formerly an important marine board site with telephone and semaphore links to the Mount Nelson maritime signal station.

'Whatever the circumstances that brought the set into Bob's possession, my clearest memories of our house at 33 Hampden Road, Battery Point, are of the shop that our mother ran during the day, and of this enormous (as it seemed to me) AWA radio. It sat on Bob's desk in his room at the top of the stairs of our small house attached to the shop on the corner of Runnymede Street.

'I was in awe of that radio. In contrast, I had been terrified by the old Ericsson telephone in the hallway of our previous home, just down the road, at Battery Square. It was an old, giant, wall-mounted device with dual bells at the top and hand-cranked line activation, which seemed to me at the time to be some kind of strange and fearful big brass-eyed monster. It gave me nightmares but was merely a telephone connection between our house and the signal station atop Mount Nelson.

'Apparently, Bob used to call the signal station using this now otherwise derelict piece of equipment and became friends with the maritime staff up there. Doubtless, this contributed to his interest in shortwave radio and he became quite adept at the business of tuning into coastal radio stations and ships at sea, which were still then predominantly using shortwave radio to communicate with land-based stations.

'Now, some six decades later, I am in possession of my own fully functioning, restored AWA 3BZ receiver. It's a matter for perhaps deep and intense psychoanalysis as to why I deemed it not only important to follow my elder brother's interest in the hobby, but in fact to devote most of my working life to the field of radio. But I have few regrets and doubtless, Bob would approve of my choice of career.

'My interest was further kindled as a young boy with Bob taking us younger brothers on frequent field trips to visit transmitter sites atop little-known and otherwise generally unvisited hilltops. There were also not infrequent visits to Llanherne Airport (better known now as Hobart Airport) to watch aircraft arrive and depart, and more importantly, to tune into the control tower and aeroplane communications on Bob's converted FM radio.

'It wasn't all about radio though. Other trips were made into the bush to cut firewood and regularly to Mount Field National Park. Here we would lark about in the Tyenna River, a shallow but swift-flowing white-water playground, or mess about on the open grasslands by the picnic areas. These are fond and frequent memories. Such trips continued, albeit with less frequency, after Bob married and had a family of his own. He continued, though, to look after his younger siblings in much the same way he cared for his children, that is, with genuine fondness, care and occasional warranted discipline.

'Field trips in his beloved cars continued – excursions to the motor racing, soccer matches, odd and exotic transmitter sites, the airport to watch/listen to the aircraft, and the Post Office Museum in Salamanca Place were frequent and keenly

Me at the age of five with Bob and Mary at their wedding. Perhaps I was only too aware of being about to lose my big brother.

attended. Visits to various beaches were also common – Carlton Beach, Seven Mile Beach and Nutgrove Beach being chief among them.

'Looking back now, I am amazed at the number of small but significant trips we undertook as siblings, despite the fact that when I was a mere five years old, Bob married Mary and was no longer living in the same house. Yet somehow, even as he raised his own family, he found time for his younger brothers, and those times remain fixed firmly in my memory banks as gloriously happy ones.

'His enthusiasm for radio (and anything electronic) and music naturally went hand-in-hand. His love of early 60s artists such as the Beatles, the Everly Brothers, Gene Pitney and countless others also played a big part in my own musical tastes. My own habit of listening to distant Top 40 stations on my little 9-transistor, powder blue radio late at night quietly impressed him. My unfortunate habit of draining expensive 9-volt batteries by falling asleep with the 'trannie' surreptitiously chirruping away under my pillow at night (much to the displeasure of our mother) was occasionally bolstered with the gift of a replacement battery from Bob. Then, when one day he presented me with a portable record player – my first such prized possession – which he had himself repaired to working condition, it seemed as if all my Christmases had come at once, and I treasured that record player for a great many years.

'His all-too-sudden departure from the mortal realm at just 30 years of age was a shock to the system which I am sure none of us ever properly recovered from. I was utterly unable to process what his death actually meant. In practical terms what it did for me, as an otherwise scholastic student then in year 10, was to abandon my desire to go to university for a career in science, and instead take on an unfulfilling job in a bank that was to last a mere 18 months. Only by complete chance did I end up working in radio – although as I write that, one has to wonder if such strange circumstances ever happen completely by chance. In any event, I did eventually achieve my B.Sc. much later as an adult student, something I think Bob would be quite pleased about.

'Despite our significant age gap, Bob's influence on me was profound, as I'm pretty sure it would have been on everyone he ever encountered. He was such a loveable larrikin who loved life to the full and – in my presence at least – never had a bad word to say about anyone or anything. For him, life was for living, and in his short allotted span he undoubtedly did that, and that by itself is an inspiration for us all.'

◆

7. 9th August 1977

Mary:

'Now, that fateful day. As mentioned before, when he was on holidays, days off or afternoon/night shift, he would take the boys to school. Bags packed, Cameron in his stroller and off they went. It was a beautiful sunny day, and on his return, he suggested we go for a picnic. Bob hadn't worn a watch for some time and for an unknown reason my watch stopped working. To figure out what time to pick up the boys, we decided to take a $5 trannie with us. Picnic lunch packed, and finally on our way to Lane Cove National Park. Bob convinced me to take a canoe trip; I was against it as Cameron was only 12 months old. To this day, I do not know why I didn't refuse this request.

'We packed everything into the canoe, and off we set to this lovely area. Next, Bob realised the trannie was missing, so he returned to the car. Once again, why did I not say forget it? All will be fine! He seemed to be taking his time. Cameron was getting hungry and restless. He was fed up with playing with toys in his trolley. The paddle steamer came into view, and after that, we watched an outboard dinghy coming towards us. My stomach clenched, and I felt sick (I am feeling it now). I couldn't breathe, and my heart stopped. Something was wrong. The police asked me many questions; everyone was very kind and solicitous. A policewoman looked after Cameron while I answered more questions.

'They informed Dad, who immediately told Mum and John. John and Robyn were back in Sydney. Cameron and I were taken to Mum's home. The boys were picked up from school. The rest is a blank. I was swayed not to see him, and to this very day, I wish I had been more forceful about the viewing and allowing the boys to attend the funeral. It wasn't until months later that I found out the true story.

'He did not have a diabetic seizure, as we were led to believe. I and the funeral company established a group for young widows and widowers. I was being interviewed on radio about this group when we detoured to the funeral home. I met this wonderful Irishman who told me Bob did not have a chance. He was seen swimming towards the shore. I knew this as five or six people saw him, then he disappeared. They thought he had reached the shore. This fellow told me that he was so interested in Bob's case as it was similar to one he had in Ireland.

'In both cases, there was evidence of weeds/reeds wrapped around his legs, and no matter how hard he tried to swim or unwrap himself, he was pulled under. Once he had stopped struggling, the weeds eventually released their grip. His body then drifted down to the weir, where he was found. Now I knew the true story, and finally, after several years, I returned to this beautiful park. It wasn't as bad as I thought. Unfortunately, my brain has blocked out the years following his death. I feel so remorseful for the boys as I cannot remember how our lives endured during this time.

'A couple of weeks after Bob's death, it was the boys' soccer presentation. Eric was able to see his grandsons receive their trophies. One year that Bob wasn't working. Both teams were very successful this year. My Dad had coached a team this year, and while he was awarding his boys, he broke down. He and Bob occasionally discussed coaching techniques etc. The coaches, managers and president of Ryde RSL Junior Sports paid tribute to Bob. He would have been so embarrassed but very proud.'

Peter:

'In 1977, the first family tragedy that affected me personally occurred. On 9 August, Bob died. It's been said that no man can lose anyone closer than a brother, and I'm inclined to agree. Our age difference meant we were never as close as most brothers appear to be, but his loss was no less diminished for that. I'm forced to concede now that I have sat in the front at too many funerals. Bob's was the first, and they don't get any easier.

'I recall very little of the trip we took to Sydney for the funeral, and imagine now that I was too traumatised to take it all in. Bob's brother-in-law, John Fitzgerald, in particular, was very good to us, and I will always be grateful for that. Mary had the worst of it, of course, especially as they had just had their third son, Cameron, who was mercifully too young to realise what was happening.

'The day of the funeral was unpleasant weather-wise, and that just added to a thoroughly unpleasant day. I was pleased to get back home.'[19]

◆

---

19 *Twenty-Five Years*, ISBN 978-0-9873470-5-3

8. Some Random Memories

Another digression: Peter and Graham hesitated to ask for input from Mary and the boys when contemplating this book. They thought it might be traumatic for Mary and that Andrew and Brian's memories may be too vague, as they were very young when their father died. Cameron, of course, was not quite a year old and far too young to remember. Mary confessed that detailing her life with Bob was distressing but was a positive experience and 'lifted a weight'.

Andrew and Brian dredged their memories and provided some insights into growing up with their father. The following, necessarily random memories, are presented here as they couldn't be readily included in the book's main narrative.

Andrew

- There were times when Mum and Dad would go to parties, and Brian and I would go, but at a certain point, we would have to go and sleep in the car because it was getting late, probably 7:00 pm.
- I remember heading into the bush with a car, trailer and chainsaw in the cold and wet, and I still enjoy it on days like that.
- Living above the Basin in Launceston and walking down the bush path at the end of Quarry Road to the Basin, which Lana and I did on our honeymoon – and well done, Mum and Dad, dealing with Brian and me at such a young age on that walk.
- Drives to and from the hospital, picking up Mum after work and Dad not allowing Brian and me to have ice cream because one of us would not correct ourselves and say finger instead of 'thinger'. The weird things that you remember even 50 years later. Traumatised for life, I guess.
- Visits to Burnie to visit Mum's best friend, Jill.
- Watching the horse racing from the roadside, might have only done it once, but I still remember it strongly.
- Visits to Batman Bridge and a trip to Low Head Lighthouse.
- Walking through City Park in Launceston and the conservatory.

- Of course, there were multiple trips to Symmons Plains, with memories or moments going through my mind during the drive on the Midland Highway heading south as you approached the racetrack.
- I remember family drives to Hobart and visits to Mount Wellington, especially one very cold, wet and windy day. Visits to Constitution Dock and Princes Park at Battery Point, but other than that, I have no strong memories.
- I don't really remember much in the way of specifics other than those things, and Low Head is only a recent memory as we went there on our honeymoon, and I had one of those flashback moments realising that I had been there before.

Brian

- The only thing I have of Dad's is his wedding ring. About eight years ago, Mum randomly asked if I had anything. I said no and thought that that was it for the conversation. She returned a few minutes later and just gave me his wedding ring. I suppose it was because Cameron's engagement ring for Danielle was Mum's from Dad, and she thought I should have something. I presume that Andrew has some stuff as well. He and Cameron have had more chances to go through whatever has been kept over time.
- I don't remember much of anything, really, apart from climbing in and out of the Land Rover. We got stranded in a swollen river once in the outback and got dragged out by a conveniently nearby grader. Maybe Dad called them up on the CB to save us, but I don't know.
- Same trip, I presume; pretty sure we had to race a summer storm over the mountains to get home before it hit.
- I remember we bought a car (a little Mazda van, maybe?) from somewhere on Parramatta Road.
- There are a few memories of William Street, Ryde, but, to be honest, that's more because one of my closest friends, someone I've known for maybe 47 years, lived one street over.
- Thinking about it, things I remember from back then don't really have Dad as part of them. Or, more accurately, I just don't picture

- him being there, although obviously, he was. I presume that's a coping mechanism, and I'm sure there's some physiological reasoning to it.
- Remember being at Chulora Railway yards one day with him and Andrew. Don't know if it was train spotting or listening in to railway radio communications, but I'm sure I have an interest in funky jazz-inspired late 70s style music because of that day. (Jamiroquai, anyone?) Honestly could be some random Stevie Wonder or similar song that came on the radio, but it's always stuck in my mind.
- Mum (being a typical Mum) once asked me if there was something I was searching for, re my travels, living overseas, not married, moving around etc.
- To be honest, that's just how I've chosen to live. I enjoy experiencing new things and different environments. Is it a genetic thing or, again, a physiological coping mechanism? It is something that I've thought about over the years. But, I suppose, when something like your father dies when you're age seven, it's natural to look forward, not back.
- I've always gone with the genetics answer. More than one person has asked if I'm part gypsy.
- Anyway, as I said, I don't remember much, but that's not to say that he's forgotten. It's just that I look at taking whatever positives can be had from anything that life throws at you, and if my brain chooses not to remember experiences that could be upsetting, then so be it.
- So, things that I remember that my dad liked. Road trips, trains (we had a huge collection of train magazines for ages at Eileen Street), radio communications (something Andrew was certainly more interested in). He and Uncle John had a sideline thing building and selling bunk beds out of granddads garage.

From Graham: discussion with Brian

- On the day of Bob's death, he remembers only being collected from school by John (I presumed Uncle John, not Grandpa Jack) and being taken to their favourite nearby park, where the boys were told what had happened. Being only seven at the time, he couldn't

- process it, not understanding what any of it meant, and it took some time to properly sink in.
- He has some memories of Bob's radio habit, which apparently Andrew took on after Bob's death. He recollects the Yaesu FRG-7 quite well, but the rest of it (aircraft, CB etc.) means nothing to him. Similarly, the stamp-collecting hobby meant nothing to him, but he clearly remembers Bob's love of cars and driving.

Peter

- 'When Bob and Mary were (as the old saying goes) courting, one day they announced their intention to go to a beach, probably Sandy Bay Beach. Naturally, I thought it only right and proper that they should take me. But, equally naturally, they didn't want to. It was a shattering rejection for me, but I have now forgiven them.'

◆

9. A Final Word from Mary

'Bob and I had a wonderful relationship. He was not only protective and attentive but very caring towards the children and me. He was a kind, loving man, although didn't often show this side of himself to others. Sometimes he was quite reserved. We rarely had differences of opinion – we agreed to disagree. A good caring Dad, firm (at times, I thought too firm) but fair. After he died, I tried to continue in this manner, especially bringing up three boys on my own.'

◆

10. A Final Word from Bob

Bob had a refined sense of humour. He and his friend, John (Mary's brother), would amuse us with their impressions of Peter Cook and Dudley Moore doing their on-stage personas, Pete and Dud. Bob sent this delightful card to Mary for no apparent reason, demonstrating that sense of humour.

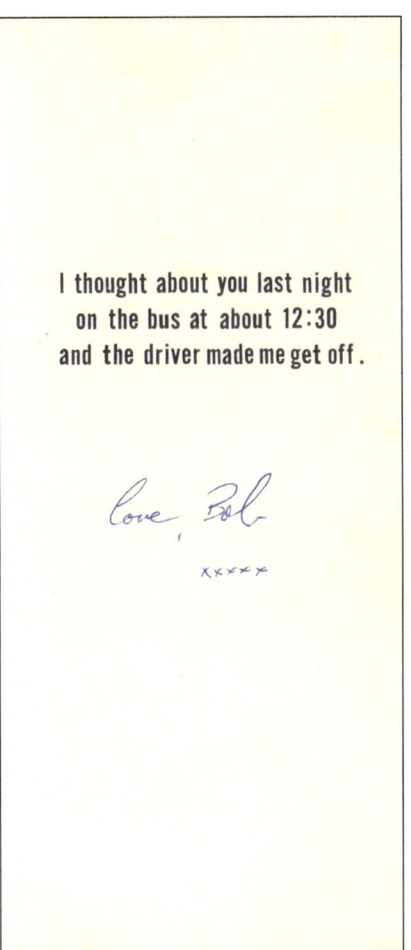

Images courtesy Hallmark Australia.

11. Some Random Photos

In the course of compiling this small volume and illustrating it with various images, several were excluded. Along the lines of Some Random Memories, some of those are presented here in the interests of a greater degree of completion.

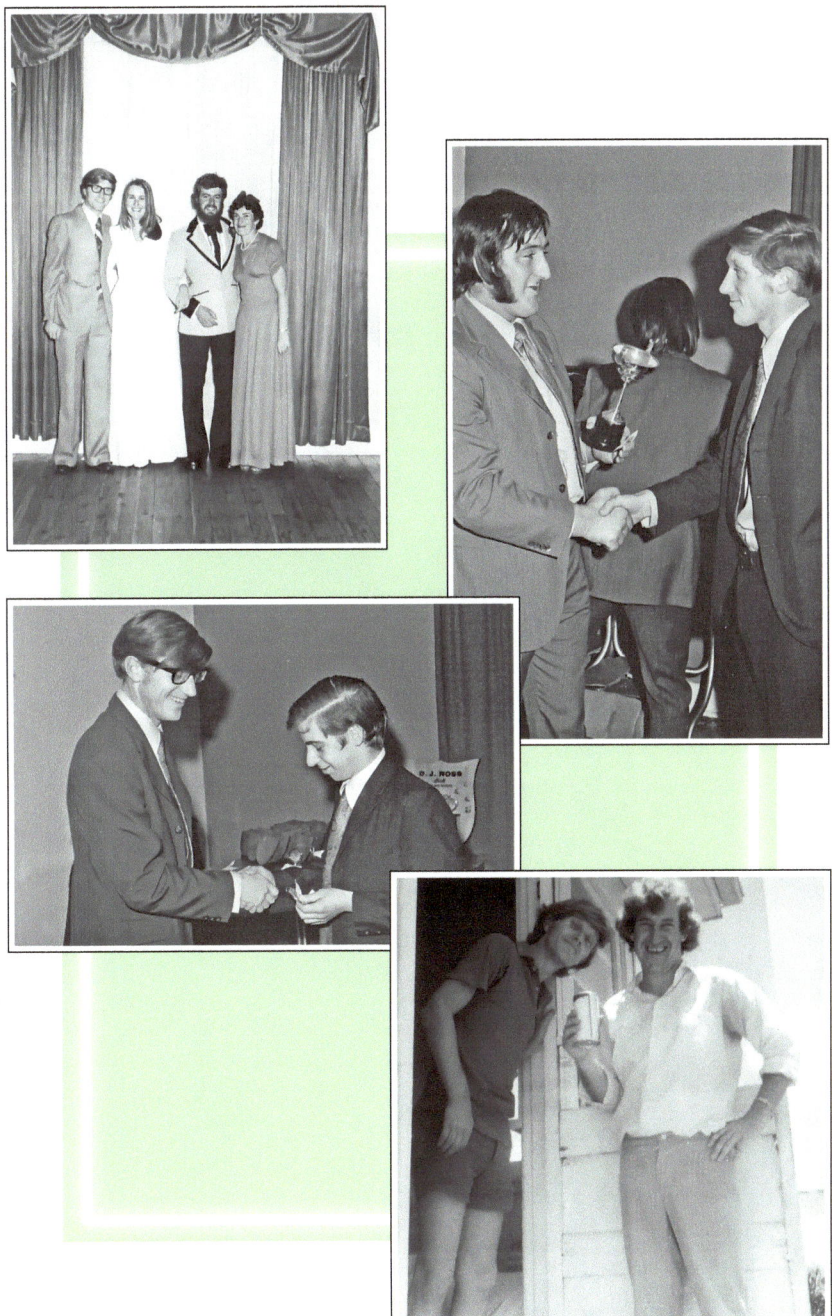

www.ingramcontent.com/pod-product-compliance
Lightning Source LLC
Chambersburg PA
CBHW041401160426
42811CB00101B/1506